AT THE HAWK'S WELL

By W. B. YEATS

A Digireads.com Book
Digireads.com Publishing

At the Hawk's Well
By W. B. Yeats
ISBN 10: 1-4209-4155-0
ISBN 13: 978-1-4209-4155-5

This edition copyright © 2011

Please visit *www.digireads.com*

PERSONS OF THE PLAY

Three Musicians [*their faces made up to resemble masks*]
The Guardian of the Well [*with face made up to resemble a mask*]
An Old Man [*wearing a mask*]
A Young Man [*wearing a mask*]

The Time—the Irish Heroic Age.

The stage is any bare space before a wall against which stands a patterned screen. A drum and a gong and a zither have been laid close to the screen before the play begins. If necessary, they can be carried in, after the audience is seated, by the First Musician, who also can attend to the lights if there is any special lighting. We had two lanterns upon posts—designed by Mr. Dulac—at the outer corners of the stage, but they did not give enough light, and we found it better to play by the light of a large chandelier. Indeed I think, so far as my present experience goes, that the most effective lighting is the lighting we are most accustomed to in our rooms. These masked players seem stranger' when there is no mechanical means of separating them from us. The First Musician carries with him a folded black cloth and goes to the centre of the stage towards the front and stands motionless, the folded cloth hanging from between his hands. The two musicians enter and, after standing a moment at either side of the stage, go towards him and slowly unfold the cloth, singing as they do so:

> I call to the eye of the mind
> A well long choked up and dry
> And boughs long stripped by the wind,
> And I call to the mind's eye
> Pallor of an ivory face,
> Its lofty dissolute air,
> A man climbing up to a place
> The salt sea wind has swept bare.

As they unfold the cloth, they go backward a little so that the stretched cloth and the wall make a triangle with the First Musician at the apex supporting the centre of the cloth. On the black cloth is a gold pattern suggesting a hawk. The Second and Third Musicians now slowly fold up the cloth again, pacing with a rhythmic movement of the arms towards the First Musician and singing:

> What were his life soon done!
> Would he lose by that or win?
> A mother that saw her son
> Doubled over a speckled shin,
> Cross-grained with ninety years,
> Would cry, "How little worth
> Were all my hopes and fears
> And the hard pain of his birth!"

The words "a speckled shin" are familiar to readers of Irish legendary stories in descriptions of old men bent double over the fire. While the cloth has been spread out, the Guardian of the Well has entered and is now crouching upon the ground. She is entirely covered by a black cloak. The three musicians have taken their places against the wall beside their instruments of music; they will accompany the movements of the players with gong or drum or zither.

FIRST MUSICIAN. [*singing*]
    The boughs of the hazel shake,
    The sun goes down in the west.

SECOND MUSICIAN. [*singing*]
    The heart would be always awake,
    The heart would turn to its rest.

[*They now go to one side of the stage rolling up the cloth.*]

FIRST MUSICIAN. [*speaking*] Night falls;
    The mountain-side grows dark;
    The withered leaves of the hazel
    Half-choke the dry bed of the well;
    The guardian of the well is sitting
    Upon the old grey stone at its side,
    Worn out from raking its dry bed,
    Worn out from gathering up the leaves.
    Her heavy eyes
    Know nothing, or but look upon stone.
    The wind that blows out of the sea
    Turns over the heaped-up leaves at her side;
    They rustle and diminish.

SECOND MUSICIAN. I am afraid of this place.

BOTH MUSICIANS. [*singing*]
        "Why should I sleep," the heart cries,
        "For the wind, the salt wind, the sea wind
        Is beating a cloud through the skies;
        I would wander always like the wind."

[*An Old Man enters through the audience.*]

FIRST MUSICIAN. [*speaking*] That old man climbs up hither,
Who has been watching by his well
These fifty years.
He is all doubled up with age;
The old thorn-trees are doubled so
Among the rocks where he is climbing.

[*The Old Man stands for a moment motionless by the side of the stage with bowed head. He lifts his head at the sound of a drum tap. He goes towards the front of the stage moving to the taps of the drum. He crouches and moves his hands as if making a fire. His movements, like those of the other persons of the play, suggest a marionette.*]

FIRST MUSICIAN. [*speaking*] He has made a little heap of leaves;
He lays the dry sticks on the leaves
And, shivering with cold, he has taken up
The fire-stick and socket from its hole.
He whirls it round to get a flame;
And now the dry sticks take the fire
And now the fire leaps up and shines
Upon the hazels and the empty well.

MUSICIANS. [*singing*]
"O wind, O salt wind, O sea wind!"
Cries the heart, "it is time to sleep;
Why wander and nothing to find?
Better grow old and sleep."

OLD MAN. [*speaking*] Why don't you speak to me? Why
   don't you say:
  "Are you not weary gathering those sticks?
  Are not your fingers cold?" You have not one word,
  While yesterday you spoke three times. You said:
  "The well is full of hazel leaves." You said:
  "The wind is from the west." And after that:
  "If there is rain it's likely there'll be mud."
  To-day you are as stupid as a fish,
  No, worse, worse, being less lively and as dumb.

[*He goes nearer.*]

  Your eyes are dazed and heavy. If the Sidhe
  Must have a guardian to clean out the well
  And drive the cattle off, they might choose somebody
  That can be pleasant and companionable
  Once in the day. Why do you stare like that?
  You had that glassy look about the eyes
  Last time it happened. Do you know anything?
  It is enough to drive an old man crazy
  To look all day upon these broken rocks,
  And ragged thorns, and that one stupid face,
  And speak and get no answer.

YOUNG MAN. [*who has entered through the audience
   during the last speech*]
  Then speak to me,
  For youth is not more patient than old age;
  And though I have trod the rocks for half a day
  I cannot find what I am looking for.

OLD MAN. Who speaks?
>   Who comes so suddenly into this place
>   Where nothing thrives? If I may judge by the gold
>   On head and feet and glittering in your coat,
>   You are not of those who hate the living world.

YOUNG MAN. I am named Cuchulain, I am Sualtam's son.

OLD MAN. I have never heard that name.

CUCHULAIN. It is not unknown.
>   I have an ancient house beyond the sea.

OLD MAN. What mischief brings you hither?—you are like those
>   Who are crazy for the shedding of men's blood,
>   And for the love of women?

YOUNG MAN. A rumour has led me,
>   A story told over the wine towards dawn.
>   I rose from table, found a boat, spread sail
>   And with a lucky wind under the sail
>   Crossed waves that have seemed charmed, and found this shore.

OLD MAN. There is no house to sack among these hills
>   Nor beautiful woman to be carried off.

YOUNG MAN. You should be native here, for that rough
        tongue
    Matches the barbarous spot. You can, it may be,
    Lead me to what I seek, a well wherein
    Three hazels drop their nuts and withered leaves,
    And where a solitary girl keeps watch
    Among grey boulders. He who drinks, they say,
    Of that miraculous water lives for ever.

OLD MAN. And are there not before your eyes at the
        instant
    Grey boulders and a solitary girl
    And three stripped hazels?

YOUNG MAN. But there is no well.

OLD MAN. Can you see nothing yonder?

YOUNG MAN. I but see
    A hollow among stones half-full of leaves.

OLD MAN. And do you think so great a gift is found
    By no more toil than spreading out a sail,
    And climbing a steep hill? Oh, folly of youth,
    Why should that hollow place fill up for you,
    That will not fill for me ? I have lain in wait
    For more than fifty years to find it empty,
    Or but to find the stupid wind of the sea
    Drive round the perishable leaves.

YOUNG MAN. So it seems
    There is some moment when the water fills it.

OLD MAN. A secret moment that the holy shades
    That dance upon the desolate mountain know,
    And not a living man, and when it comes
    The water has scarce plashed before it is gone.

YOUNG MAN. I will stand here and wait. Why should the luck
    Of Sualtam's son desert him now? For never
    Have I had long to wait for anything.

OLD MAN. No! Go from this accursed place, this place
    Belongs to me, that girl there and those others,
    Deceivers of men.

YOUNG MAN. And who are you who rail
    Upon those dancers that all others bless?

OLD MAN. One whom the dancers cheat. I came like you
    When young in body and in mind, and blown
    By what had seemed to me a lucky sail.
    The well was dry, I sat upon its edge,
    I waited the miraculous flood, I waited
    While the years passed and withered me away.
    I have snared the birds for food and eaten grass
    And drunk the rain, and neither in dark nor shine
    Wandered too far away to have heard the plash,
    And yet the dancers have deceived me. Thrice
    I have awakened from a sudden sleep
    To find the stones were wet.

YOUNG MAN. My luck is strong,
    It will not leave me waiting, nor will they
    That dance among the stones put me asleep;
    If I grow drowsy I can pierce my foot.

OLD MAN. No, do not pierce it, for the foot is tender,
   It feels pain much. But find your sail again
   And leave the well to me, for it belongs
   To all that's old and withered.

YOUNG MAN. No, I stay.

   [*The Girl gives the cry of the hawk.*]

   There is that bird again.

OLD MAN. There is no bird.

YOUNG MAN. It sounded like the sudden cry of a hawk,
   But there's no wing in sight. As I came hither
   A great grey hawk swept down out of the sky,
   And though I have good hawks, the best in the world
   I had fancied, I have not seen its like. It flew
   As though it would have torn me with its beak,
   Or blinded me, smiting with that great wing.
   I had to draw my sword to drive it off,
   And after that it flew from rock to rock.
   I pelted it with stones, a good half-hour,
   And just before I had turned the big rock there
   And seen this place, it seemed to vanish away.
   Could I but find a means to bring it down
   I'd hood it.

OLD MAN. The woman of the Sidhe herself,
   The mountain witch, the unappeasable shadow,
   She is always flitting upon this mountain-side,
   To allure or to destroy. When she has shown
   Herself to the fierce women of the hills
   Under that shape they offer sacrifice

And arm for battle. There falls a curse
On all who have gazed in her unmoistened eyes;
So get you gone while you have that proud step
And confident voice, for not a man alive
Has so much luck that he can play with it.
Those that have long to. live should fear her most,
The old are cursed already. That curse may be
Never to win a woman's love and keep it;
Or always to mix hatred in the love;
Or it may be that she will kill your children,
That you will find them, their throats torn and bloody,
Or you will be so maddened that you kill them
With your own hand.

YOUNG MAN. Have you been set down there
To threaten all who come, and scare them off?
You seem as dried up as the leaves and sticks,
As though you had no part in life.

[*Girl gives hawk cry again.*]

That cry!
There is that cry again. That woman made it,
But why does she cry out as the hawk cries?

OLD MAN. It was her mouth, and yet not she, that cried.
It was that shadow cried behind her mouth;
And now I know why she has been so stupid
All the day through, and had such heavy eyes.
Look at her shivering now, the terrible life
Is slipping through her veins. She is possessed.
Who knows whom she will murder or betray
Before she awakes in ignorance of it all,
And gathers up leaves! But they'll be wet;
The water will have come and gone again;

That shivering is the sign. Oh, get you gone,
At any moment now I shall hear it bubble.
If you are good you will leave it. I am old,
And if I do not drink it now, will never;
I have been watching all my life and maybe
Only a little cupful will bubble up.

YOUNG MAN. I'll take it in my hands. We shall both drink,
And even if there are but a few drops,
Share them.

OLD MAN. But swear that I may drink the first;
The young are greedy, and if you drink the first
You'll drink it all. Ah, you have looked at her;
She has felt your gaze and turned her eyes on us;
I cannot bear her eyes, they are not of this world,
Nor moist, nor faltering; they are no girl's eyes.

[*He covers his head. The Guardian of the Well throws of her cloak and rises. Her dress under the cloak suggests a hawk.*]

YOUNG MAN. Why do you gaze upon me with the eyes of a hawk?
I am not afraid of you, bird, woman, or witch.

[*He goes to the side of the well, which the Guardian of the Well has left.*]

Do what you will, I shall not leave this place
Till I have grown immortal like yourself.

[*He has sat down, the Girl has begun to dance, moving like a hawk. The Old Man sleeps. The dance goes on for some time.*]

FIRST MUSICIAN. [*singing or half-singing*]
> O God protect me
> From a horrible deathless body
> Sliding through the veins of a sudden.

[*The dance goes on for some time. The Young Man rises slowly.*]

FIRST MUSICIAN. [*speaking*] The madness has laid hold upon him now,
For he grows pale and staggers to his feet.

[*The dance goes on.*]

YOUNG MAN. Run where you will,
Grey bird, you shall be perched upon my wrist,
Some were called queens and yet have been perched there.

[*The dance goes on.*]

FIRST MUSICIAN. [*speaking*] I have heard water plash; it comes, it comes;
It glitters among the stones and he has heard the plash;
Look, he has turned his head.

[*The Hawk has gone out. The Young Man drops his spear as if in a dream and goes out.*]

MUSICIANS. [*singing*] He has lost what may not be found

> Till men heap his burial mound
> And all the history ends.
> He might have lived at his ease,
> An old dog's head on his knees,
> Among his children and friends.

[*The Old Man creeps up to the well.*]

OLD MAN. The accursed shadows have deluded me,
   The stones are dark and yet the well is empty;
   The water flowed and emptied while I slept;
   You have deluded me my whole life through.
   Accursed dancers, you have stolen my life.
   That there should be such evil in a shadow.

YOUNG MAN. [*entering*] She has fled from me and hidden in the rocks.

OLD MAN. She has but led you from the fountain. Look!
   The stones and leaves are dark where it has flowed,
   Yet there is not a drop to drink.

[*The Musicians cry "Aoife!" " Aoife" and strike gong.*]

YOUNG MAN. What are those cries?
   What is that sound that runs along the hill?
   Who are they that beat a sword upon a shield?

OLD MAN. She has roused up the fierce women of the hills,
Aoife, and all her troop, to take your life,
And never till you are lying in the earth,
Can you know rest.

YOUNG MAN. The clash of arms again!

OLD MAN. Oh, do not go! The mountain is accursed;
Stay with me, I have nothing more to lose,
I do not now deceive you.

YOUNG MAN. I will face them.

[*He goes out no longer as if in a dream, but shouldering his spear and calling*]

He comes! Cuchulain, son of Sualtam, comes!

[*The Musicians stand up, one goes to centre with folded cloth. The others unfold it. While they do so they sing. During the singing, and while hidden by the cloth, the Old Man goes out. When the play is performed with Mr. Dulac's music, the Musicians do not rise or unfold the cloth till after they have sung the words "a bitter life."*]

[*Songs for the unfolding and folding of the cloth.*]

Come to me, human faces,
Familiar memories;
I have found hateful eyes
Among the desolate places,
Unfaltering, unmoistened eyes.

Folly alone I cherish,
I choose it for my share,
Being but a mouthful of air,
I am content to perish,
I am but a mouthful of sweet air.

O lamentable shadows,
Obscurity of strife,
I choose a pleasant life,
Among indolent meadows;
Wisdom must live a bitter life.

[*They then fold up the cloth, again singing.*]

"The man that I praise,"
Cries out the empty well,
"Lives all his days
Where a hand on the bell
Can call the milch cows
To the comfortable door of his house.
Who but an idiot would praise
Dry stones in a well?"

"The man that I praise,"
Cries out the leafless tree,
"Has married and stays
By an old hearth, and he
On naught has set store
But children and dogs on the floor.
Who but an idiot would praise
A withered tree?"

[*They go out.*]

Lightning Source UK Ltd.
Milton Keynes UK
UKHW040713050320
359822UK00001B/6